The Rainy Day

By Donna Latham

Illustrated by Aleksey Ivanov

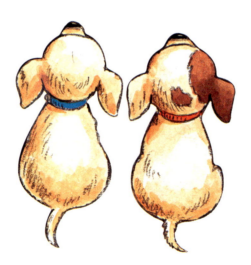

Target Skill Consonant Ll /l/

Scott Foresman
is an imprint of

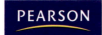

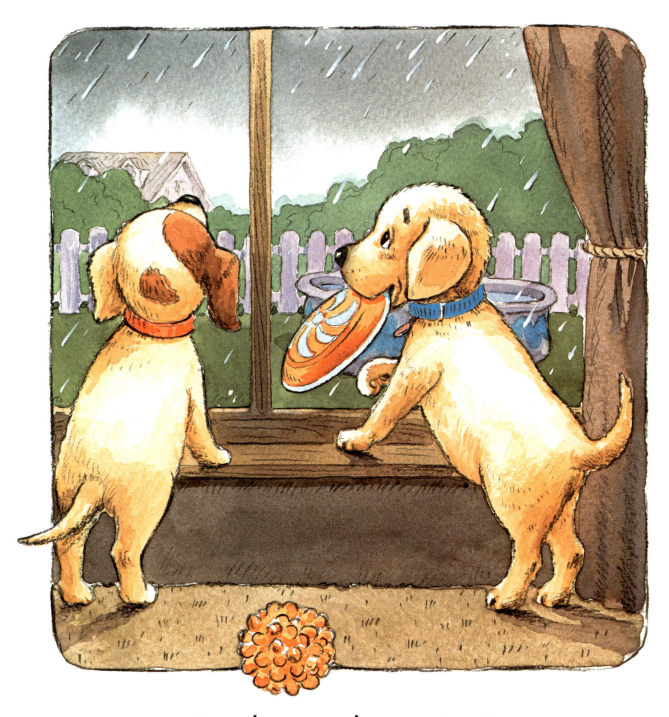

Look at that, Lin!

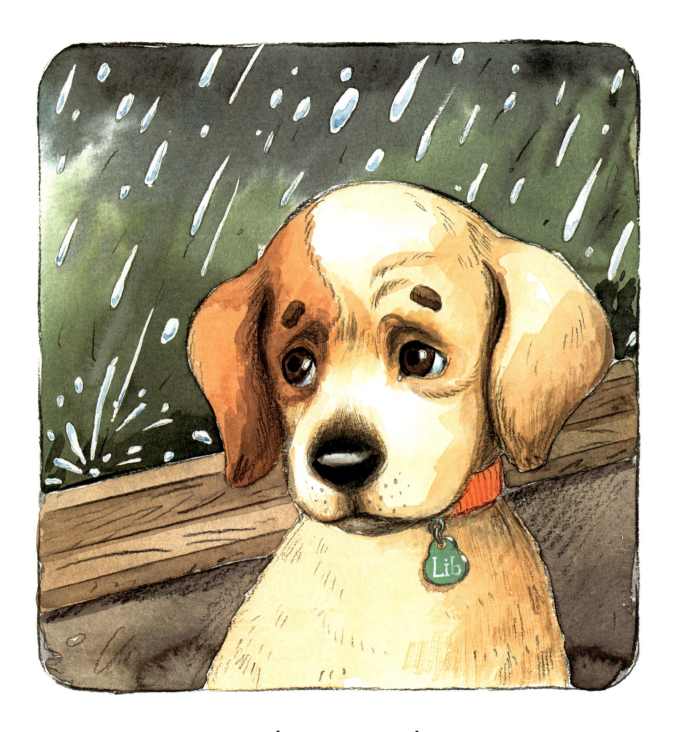

Lib is sad.

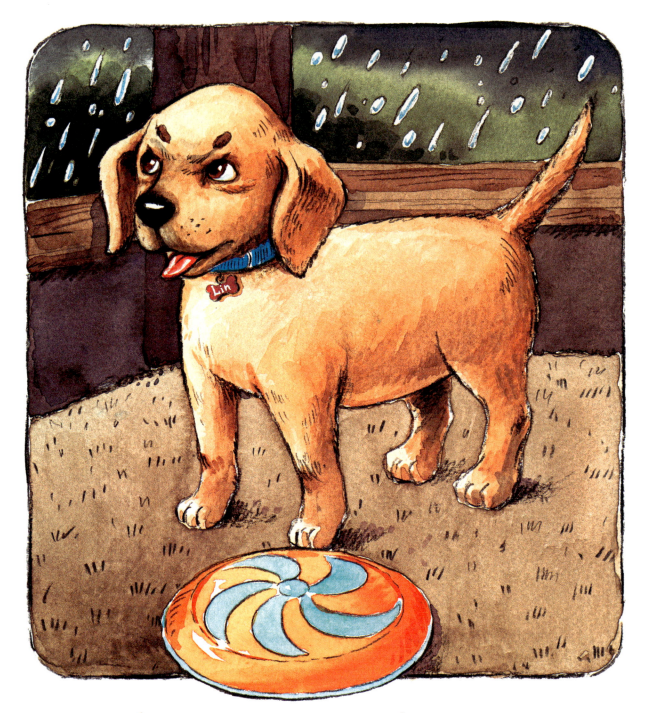

Lin is mad.

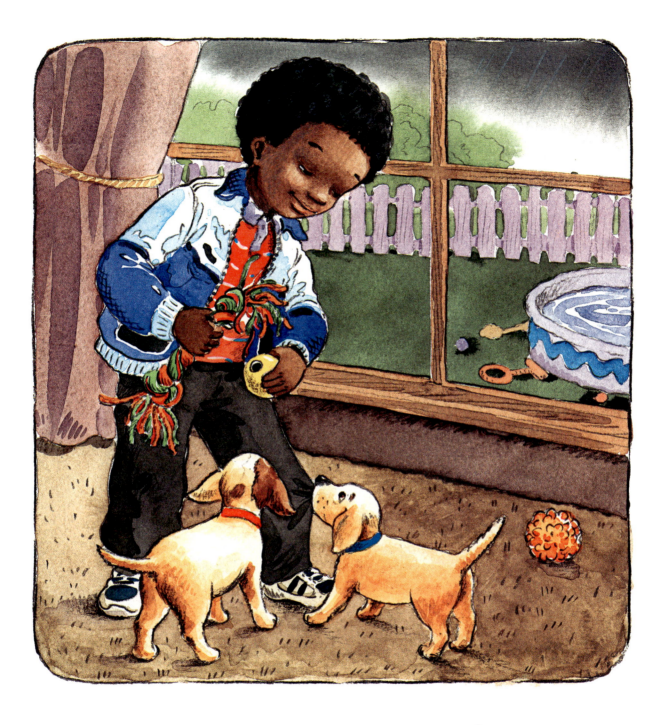

Do you see it, Rob?

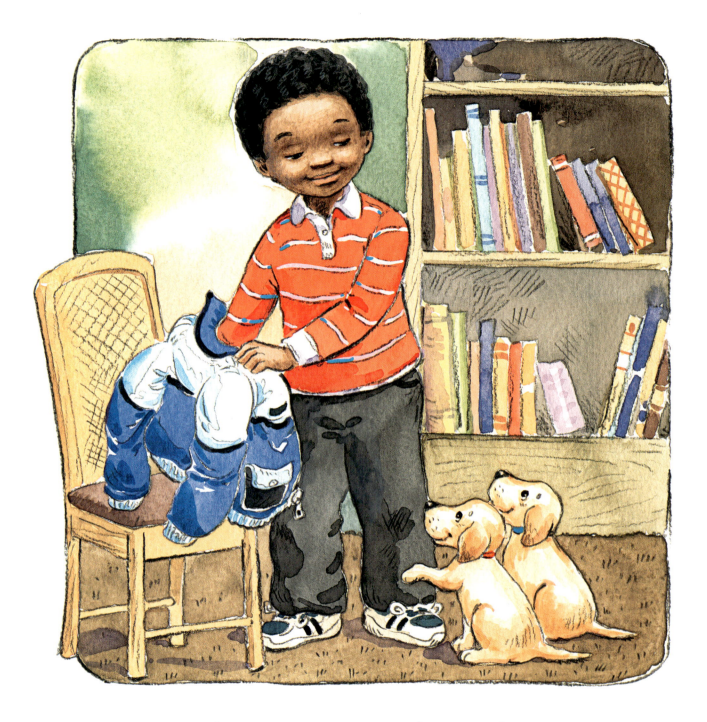

Are you sad, Rob?

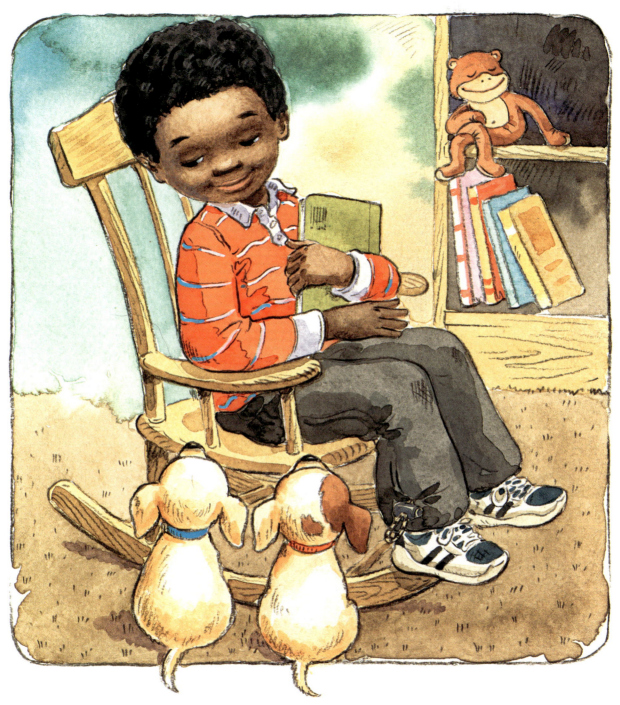

Hop on my lap.

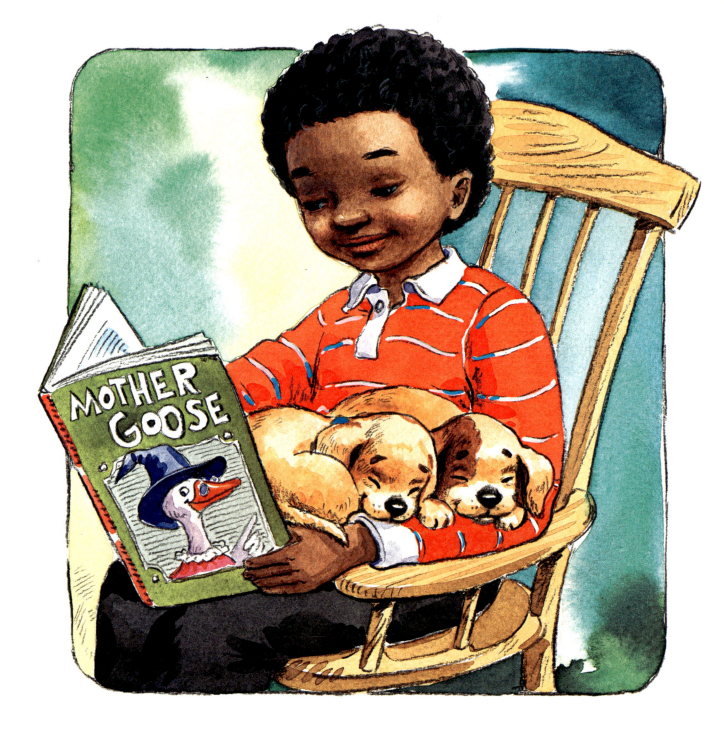

Lin and Lib nap!